FLOOD
THE WORLD REACTS

Paul Bennett

Chrysalis Children's Books

FOREWORD

Disasters affect everyone. At some point in your life, you have a good chance of being caught in one or of knowing somebody who is caught in one.

For most of us, the disaster may be a car crash or a house fire, and the police, fire or ambulance service will be on hand to help. But for millions of people around the world, disasters happen far more often and are more catastrophic.

Some countries suffer frequent natural disasters, such as floods, earthquakes and droughts. They do not always have the resources to deal with the crisis and it is usually the poorest people who are the most affected and least able to recover.

War is a human-made disaster that ruins people's lives. The effects of droughts and floods are made worse when there is war.

When people find they are unable to cope with a disaster, they need the help of aid agencies, such as the Red Cross.

Aid agencies react quickly to emergencies, bringing help to those in need. Usually it is when this international aid begins to flow that you hear about a disaster in the news.

The World Reacts series ties in closely with the work of the International Federation of Red Cross and Red Crescent Societies. The Federation coordinates international disaster relief and promotes development around the world, to prevent and alleviate human suffering. There is a Red Cross or Red Crescent society in almost every country of the world. Last year we helped 22 million people caught up in disaster.

This series will help you to understand the problems faced by people threatened by disaster and to see how you can help. We hope that you enjoy these books.

George Weber
Secretary General, International Federation of Red Cross and Red Crescent Societies

◀ *The Red Cross symbol (left) was first created to protect the wounded in war and those who cared for them. The Red Crescent symbol (right) is used by Muslim countries around the world. Both symbols have equal status.*

CONTENTS

Words in **bold** appear in the glossary on page 31.

WHAT ARE FLOODS?

A flood happens when water from rivers or seas spills over on to dry land. A serious flood may put people's lives and property at risk.

Wet weather

The main cause of flooding is extreme weather conditions. Heavy rain swells rivers and makes them burst their banks. In mountainous areas, snow melts in the spring, filling rivers and streams with water. Floods in coastal areas are mainly caused by tropical storms. These storms create huge waves, called storm surges, which flood low-lying areas.

Natural disasters

Floods also happen as a result of natural disasters, such as tsunamis and **landslides**. Earthquakes on the sea floor create huge waves, called tsunamis, which travel across the sea at great speed and pound shorelines hundreds of kilometres away. Landslides carry everything in their path down a hillside. The **debris** from the slide may block a river, causing it to burst its banks.

▼ *People wade through a flooded street in Wuxi City in China after torrential rain.*

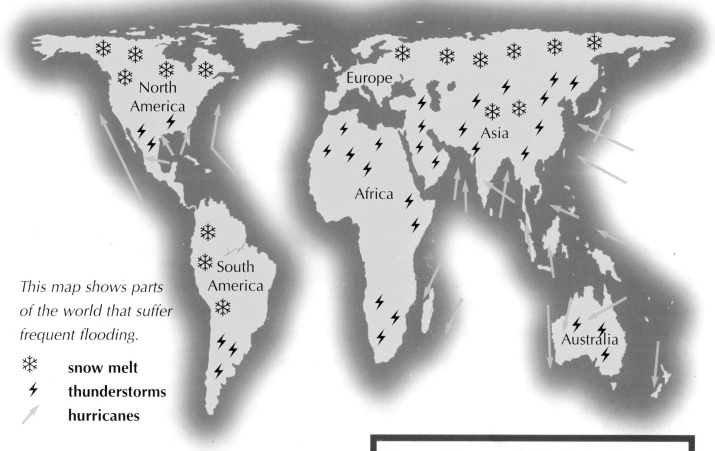

This map shows parts of the world that suffer frequent flooding.

※   **snow melt**

ϟ   **thunderstorms**

↗   **hurricanes**

Frequent floods

In some parts of the world, floods are helpful, because they make the soil fertile for farming. For example, Egyptian farmers have relied on the flooding of the River Nile to grow their crops for thousands of years.

In other parts of the world, floods are a constant threat. They cause lots of damage and threaten people's lives.

The risk of flooding can be reduced by raising river banks or building flood barriers. But it is expensive to build flood defences. Many of the countries most at risk from flooding do not have the money to build these defences. Some of the worst flood disasters have happened in the world's poorest countries.

The world maps used in this book are Peters' projection maps. Peters' projection – named after Arno Peters who made the map – is an accurate way of seeing the world, because it shows the actual size of countries.

Aid in action

Flood: The World Reacts looks at the disastrous effects a flood can have on towns and cities. It takes examples of floods from around the world and describes the help given by governments and **aid agencies**.

This book will help you understand the problems people face in the days, weeks and months after a flood. It will show you how the world helps flood victims and suggests how you too can help.

RIVERS IN FLOOD

People who live near rivers are familiar with the threat of floods caused by heavy rains. From time to time this flooding causes widespread damage.

Heavy rains

When rain falls on the land, some of the water soaks into the soil and some of it runs off the surface into rivers.

When rainwater is heavy and falls over a long period of time, the river may not be wide or deep enough to carry all the water. The water rises, flows over the river's banks and floods the land.

In mountainous areas, snow falls in the winter and melts in the spring, filling streams and rivers with water. When heavy rain and a sudden thaw happen at the same time, the water level rises quickly, creating rushing **torrents** of water. There is little chance to warn people who are often unaware of the approaching flood until it is too late.

▲ *A torrent of water rushes through the village of Vaison-la-Romaine in France in 1992. More than 23 people died in the flood and the village was completely devastated.*

Wet season

In some parts of the world, the year is divided into wet and dry seasons. During the wet season, rain falls for months at a time, causing rivers to flood. In Asia, the rainy season is called monsoon. The Ganges River, which flows through India and Bangladesh, regularly floods during monsoon. People who live near it build their homes on stilts out of the reach of flood water (left), and farmers plant crops to suit the rise and fall of the water.

China 1996

High waters

Large areas of China were hit by severe rainstorms throughout July 1996. Many parts of the country had more than 20 centimetres of rain every day, leading to serious flooding. The Yellow River had its highest water level ever recorded. Powerful storms, called **typhoons**, brought more floods, adding to the damage and destruction.

By 8 August, an estimated 200 million people were affected by the floods. More than 8 million people left their homes, 2775 people were killed and 234 000 people were ill or injured.

The floods also destroyed the summer rice and grain harvest. With large areas of land flooded, farmers were unable to plant new crops and food shortages were expected.

▲ *Towns over a large area of China were completely devastated by torrential rain.*

▼ *Hebei Province was one of the worst affected areas. Boats were used to rescue trapped people.*

The government sent in millions of soldiers, policemen and **volunteers**. They **evacuated** people from their homes, shipped in relief supplies, worked to restore gas and electricity, and tried to control the effects of further flooding.

When the rising waters of the River Haihe threatened the northern city of Tianjin with its population of nine million, the authorities planned to blow up **dykes** to divert the rising river away from the city.

COASTAL FLOODS

Storms and high tides may lead to coastal flooding. Tsunamis caused by earthquakes on the sea bed may also flood the coast.

Storm and tide

The daily rise and fall of the sea are called tides. The tides come in and go out again because of the pull of the Moon and Sun. At certain times of the year, when the Moon and Sun pull together, tides are very high. These are called spring tides.

When there is a high tide and a storm at the same time, the sea level rises. Along low-lying coastlines, the sea floods the land, destroying homes and crops.

When an earthquake happens at sea, the water bulges up into huge waves, called tsunami. In deep water, the waves move across the ocean unseen. But as they reach the shallow coastline, they rise up into giant waves of up to 60 metres high and crash ashore, flooding large areas.

▼ *The awesome power of the sea can be seen as storm waves crash ashore.*

Storm warnings

Storms, such as cyclones, hurricanes and typhoons, whip up powerful winds and create huge waves. These waves crash ashore and flood low-lying areas. Lives and property can be saved if there is a warning that the storm is coming. Weather satellites **orbit** the Earth, taking pictures of storms as they develop (above). These satellites also have sensors that detect rain, wind strength and air temperature. From this information, weather experts can predict the direction of a storm and the areas most at risk from flooding. They can give a weather warning to prepare people for an approaching storm.

Vietnam 1997

Typhoon Linda

A delta is an area of land criss-crossed by river channels. They form where the river meets the sea. Many people make their homes near river deltas because the fishing is good and the land is fertile. The Mekong River Delta in Vietnam is a good example but, like other deltas, it is at risk from flooding from the sea.

On the night of 2 November 1997, Typhoon Linda tore through the Mekong River Delta. It swept away over 80 000 homes, killed 435 people, injured 833 and left over 3000 people missing. The typhoon was the worst to strike the area for almost 100 years. As well as damage to homes, roads, hospitals and schools, rice fields were flooded, fishing boats were sunk, and shrimp farms were destroyed.

▲ *A woman sorts through what is left of her home after Typhoon Linda swept through her village.*

▼ *Inspecting a sea dyke for damage after the storm.*

Relief supplies, including corrugated iron sheets and wooden poles for making shelters, rice, **mosquito** nets and blankets, were taken from the port of Ho Chi Minh to the delta. The supplies were then taken by boat to the communities living along the waterways of the delta. Aid agencies also helped to rebuild or strengthen 800 kilometres of sea dykes in Central and Northern Vietnam.

THE EL NIÑO EFFECT

El Niño is an ocean current which causes dramatic changes to the weather across the world, resulting in torrential rain and flooding in many countries.

Climate changes

El Niño is an ocean current that occurs every few years off the coast of Peru at Christmas. El Niño is Spanish for 'the boy', or 'the Christ child'.

The current is a movement of warm water from the western side of the Pacific Ocean to the eastern side. The storm clouds that form over the warm water near Indonesia move across the ocean to the coasts of South and Central America, causing sudden, heavy downpours.

The effects of El Niño are felt all over the world. It has caused not only floods, but also **droughts** in Africa and Australia. It was also responsible for the dry conditions that caused forest fires in Indonesia in 1997 and a choking smog that spread to the rest of the region.

Global warming

Air pollution is making the world's climate warmer. This is called global warming. Scientists agree that global warming will result in dramatic changes in the world's weather, causing drought and famine in some areas and torrential rain and flooding in others. The ice caps of the North and South Poles are slowly melting because of these changes (above). If this continues, the sea levels will rise, flooding low-lying land around the world. Global warming will also intensify the effects of El Niño, so we can expect more dramatic changes to the weather.

► *The forest fires in Indonesia in 1997 were partly the result of El Niño.*

Americas 1997–98

El Niño at work

In 1997, El Niño began unusually early. From April 1997 and through the first half of 1998, its terrible effects were felt all along the Pacific coastlines of North and South America.

Bolivia, Ecuador and Peru were very badly hit. **States of emergency** were declared after hurricanes and torrential rain swept across these countries. In Bolivia, heavy rain caused a mudslide that killed at least 40 people at a gold mine.

Heavy rain in Ecuador caused landslides which killed 100 people. Flooded rivers washed away whole villages, and bridges, roads and **sewers** were badly damaged.

In Peru, floods and mudslides affected 234 000 people, and claimed 137 lives between December 1997 and February 1998.

▲ *A mud slide swept through the town of Mokotoro in Bolivia killing at least 50 people.*

Aid in the form of clothes, blankets, tents, medicine, clean water and food was distributed to the affected people in these countries. Supplies had to be airlifted into areas cut off by flood waters. In some places aid agencies helped to strengthen flood defences which had been damaged, such as dykes, along rivers.

◄ *People in the Peruvian town of Ica wade through the deep, muddy water that flooded their homes.*

FLOOD RESPONSE

Rescue teams are sent in as soon as news of a flood breaks. If the disaster is too large for them to cope with, the government appeals for outside help.

Flash appeal

When the effects of high tides, heavy rain and powerful storms can be predicted, flood warnings can be given on radio and television. These warnings mean that people can escape to safety before the flood arrives.

But if the flood takes everyone by surprise, people may be unprepared for the rising waters. This is when most lives are at risk.

Rescue teams respond immediately. They rescue people from the water and those stranded on high ground or trapped on rooftops.

The **United Nations** (UN) and the **Red Cross** are often asked by governments for help. They play an important role in coordinating the response to a disaster and may make a flash appeal. This is an urgent call to the countries of the world to send aid supplies.

▲ *Boats were used to rescue people trapped in their homes when floods hit Texas, in the USA, in 1990.*

At greater risk

Many poor people live on the edges of large cities and use whatever materials they can gather to build their homes. These low-lying areas are often at risk of flooding. The homes and offices of the rich are built on higher ground away from the threat of flood water. When a flood strikes, the water easily carries away poor people's homes unless they are built on stilts (left).

Azerbaijan 1997
Appealing for aid

In June 1997, heavy rain caused several rivers in Azerbaijan to burst their banks. Homes in one area of the country were battered by hailstones the size of tennis balls which destroyed roofs and let rain into the buildings. The government tried to help people in the affected areas, but it had to make an appeal for international aid because of lack of resources.

A second wave of freak weather struck early in July, and over seven times the average monthly rainfall fell in just three days. This was followed by more heavy rain in August, adding to the damage already caused. Throughout the crisis, the government, the United Nations, the Red Cross and other aid agencies worked together to help people caught up in the disaster.

▲ *An old woman stands in front of her flooded home in the village of Pechnoie.*

▼ *The flooding affected not only the lives of ordinary people but also industry, when oil fields were flooded.*

The aid agencies gave out over 30 000 food parcels to elderly people, and a further 210 000 parcels were given to other flood victims. Repairs and building work to homes, hospitals, schools and other important buildings were completed with the help of money donated by the aid agencies.

THE RESCUE EFFORT

Once survivors of a flood are rescued
and taken to safety, they then need
shelter, food and dry clothes.

Reaching the victims

Rescue teams use boats to reach people stranded
by rising waters. But the boats may be small and
unable to carry many people.

Sometimes the flood waters cover hundreds of
square kilometres of land. Thousands of rescue
workers are needed to cover such a vast area.
People may have to fend for themselves until
help arrives.

Helicopters are sometimes used to pick up
survivors stranded on high ground or in the
branches of trees. Helicopters can search large
areas quickly, which makes them very useful
for directing the rescue effort and for assessing
the scale of the disaster.

While the survivors are being rescued, the
authorities set up relief camps and medical centres
where people can stay until the emergency is over
and they can return to what is left of their homes.

▲ A helicopter hovers as a person
stranded by the rising flood water
is lifted to safety.

Assessing the disaster

Aid agencies have teams of people who are specially trained to go to the scene of
an emergency and assess what is needed to help people. Once a call for help has
been received, emergency teams travel out to the disaster area. The report they
send back gives a picture of the number of people affected, the state of the roads
and rail links, and the items survivors need, such as food aid and medicines.

Poland 1997

The Oder bursts its banks

In July 1997, the River Oder burst its banks, flooding large parts of Central and eastern Europe. Poland was one of the countries worst affected. By August 1997, 55 people had died and 142 000 people had been evacuated from their homes.

The rescue operation was led by the Polish government, who sent in the army, fire service and police with **amphibious** vehicles, helicopters, planes and boats. Rescue teams also arrived from European countries, including Germany, Switzerland, the Ukraine (part of the former **Soviet Union**) and Hungary, in an international rescue effort.

▲ *The River Oder in flood. From the air you can get a good idea of the scale of the disaster.*

The suffering of the flood victims lasted well into the following year. Buildings had still not dried out. But with donations from the **European Union**, homes, schools and health centres were repaired.

Red Cross worker, Thierry Le Goff, said:

'The effects of the summer floods will be felt for years to come. Our immediate concern is that winter is coming and the most vulnerable families will not be able to return to acceptable living conditions without outside help.'

Flood damage to homes left thousands of people living in miserable conditions.

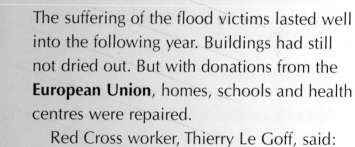

15

SHIPPING IN SUPPLIES

Aid agencies work quickly to plan the best way of sending relief supplies to the disaster area.

Transporting aid

Aid agencies have stockpiles of supplies for use in time of disaster, including tents, blankets, buckets, spades, plastic sheeting, pots and pans, electricity generators, water tanks, clothes, medical supplies and food. These are stored in huge warehouses which are often near airports, ports or railway stations.

The most urgent items, such as tents, blankets and medical supplies, are flown directly to the disaster area. But only small amounts of aid can be transported by plane – about 25 tonnes – and so many flights may be necessary.

Large ships carrying thousands of tonnes of aid may take weeks to sail to a port in the affected country. Once the ships dock, supplies are loaded on to trains or lorries.

Flood waters may have washed away bridges or damaged roads, making it difficult to deliver aid to those who need it most.

Emergency donations

Governments may send aid supplies themselves or they may donate money to aid agencies involved in the relief effort. The public may also want to give money to help flood victims. This money is spent on hiring or buying lorries; fuel for the lorries; transporting supplies by ship; helicopter services (above); repairing roads or bridges damaged in the flood; buying relief supplies; and sending aid workers to the disaster area.

◄ *In Chad, trucks carrying food cross a temporary bridge after a river washed away the bridge.*

Africa 1997–98
Sending in aid

Flooding in eastern Africa at the end of 1997 and beginning of 1998 affected large areas of Uganda, Kenya, Somalia, Ethiopia, Sudan, Djibouti and Eritrea. The region was already facing food shortages because of drought.

This crisis situation led to a huge international relief effort, involving the governments of the countries affected, the Red Cross, the United Nations and other aid agencies.

Cooperation between the countries and agencies involved was essential if the rescue effort was to be a success. For example, aid supplies shipped to the Kenyan port of Mombassa had to travel by road or rail through Kenya to reach Uganda.

▲ *The village of Rhoka in Kenya was flooded when the River Tana broke its banks.*

Roads and railways in many of the countries were damaged, and so airlifts and airdrops were often the only quick way of reaching tens of thousands of flood victims. In some areas, aid agencies used **Hercules** transport planes to fly in relief supplies until the roads were passable again. These planes flew in supplies for weeks on end. Boats were also used to reach people stranded on islands of high ground in remote areas.

◄ *Trucks make their way slowly through a flooded road in Kenya after it was blocked by heavy rain.*

FOOD SHORTAGES

A flood destroys crops and drowns farm animals. There are often food shortages after a flood which may lead to famine.

Food aid

Many people make a living from farming the land. The crops a farmer grows provide food for the family and a source of money when sold at the local market.

Floods ruin farmers' crops and food stores, leaving people without anything to eat. People sometimes lose everything they own in a flood, leaving them little to sell to buy food.

In coastal areas, a flood from the sea leaves the ground salty and unsuitable for growing crops. Eventually, the rain washes the salt away, allowing the crops to grow again, but this takes time.

People often need food aid to survive. They need emergency supplies if their food stores have been destroyed and long-term aid until the land is fit for growing again.

World Food Programme

The United Nations has a department, called the World Food Programme (WFP), which helps to coordinate food aid in emergencies. The WFP appeals to the world for food, and countries that have more than they need donate supplies. It is important that the food suits the diet of the people who need it. For example, many people in Africa and Asia eat maize or rice as their main diet. Often the WFP buys food from countries in the region where the flood has happened. This saves time and money when transporting supplies (above).

▼ *No crops can grow in this field after it was flooded by the sea.*

North Korea 1995–96

Food and floods

Flooding in North Korea in August 1995 covered one-third of the country's farmland in water and destroyed most of its crops.

The relief operation that followed included the delivery of thousands of tonnes of rice, corn and soya beans to the people most affected.

People had just begun to rebuild their lives when disaster struck again. There was more heavy rain and more flooding in July and August 1996, damaging the next harvest. The homes of nearly 150 000 people were swept away by the flood water and people faced another year of food shortages.

▲ *People receiving food aid from a WFP distribution centre in Huichon in North Korea.*

Geoff Dennis of the Red Cross surveys the damage caused by the floods.

Many people suffered from **malnutrition**, especially children. They were treated by Red Cross medical teams, as food was sent in from abroad. Red Cross representative, Geoff Dennis, who helped to run the relief operation, said:

'People lost everything. Many were rescued from higher ground, having escaped with only the clothes on their backs. The Red Cross [and other aid agencies] have carried out a remarkable job, saving lives and relieving the suffering of many people.'

DIRTY WATERS

Clean drinking water is essential for life. During a flood, streams and wells are dirtied by flood waters.

Water for life

In an emergency, it is important that survivors are provided with a supply of clean drinking water as soon as possible.

During a flood, water supplies become unclean from dirt carried in the water. Drains and sewers overflow, and the material they carry leaks into streams and wells.

Dirty water contains germs that cause disease. Cholera is a life-threatening disease that can easily be passed from person to person. In relief camps, it is important for aid agencies to set up proper toilet facilities to prevent the spread of disease.

Floods from the sea spoil water supplies. The salt has to be removed from the water before it is drinkable again.

Aid agencies help communities to clean up their water supplies and provide new sources of clean water by sinking wells.

▲ *A Bangladeshi woman stands at a well surrounded by rising flood water.*

Fighting disease

As well as treating the injured, aid agencies work to fight disease. **Médecins Sans Frontières** (MSF) sends doctors, nurses and health workers to help flood victims. Medical workers advise on setting up toilets, treat water to make it drinkable again, and give medicines to people suffering from fever, diarrhoea and other illnesses. In relief camps, disease spreads quickly between people living closely together. Medical workers can protect against some diseases by giving vaccinations – injections of medicines that will prevent flood victims from becoming ill.

DRC 1998

Preventing disease

During 1998 heavy rainfall caused the Congo River and the rivers that feed it to burst their banks and flood an area thousands of kilometres wide in the Democratic Republic of Congo (DRC). One of the worst effects of the flood was the outbreak of disease – as many as one million people were expected to fall ill because of the dirty water from the floods.

Elderly people, children, and those weak from lack of food were particularly at risk. The government and aid agencies were worried that an outbreak of cholera in Kisangani, DRC's largest northern city, would spread to other parts of the country.

Malaria was also a threat. This is a disease spread by insects called mosquitoes which breed quickly over large areas of stagnant water.

▲ *People wade through a flooded street after the Congo River burst its banks.*

▼ *A child is treated in hospital after becoming ill through drinking dirty water.*

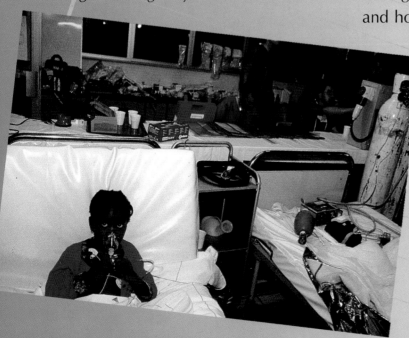

Aid agencies shipped in supplies to clinics and hospitals across the DRC, including 10 000 anti-cholera vaccines; 50 000 syringes for giving injections; 200 000 packs of salts for making special drinks for people with diarrhoea; 2000 square metres of plastic sheeting for beds; 500 large pots for boiling water; water purification tablets and 500 shovels for digging pits to bury rubbish.

DISAPPEARING FORESTS

Large numbers of trees are cut down to clear land for farming and to supply wood for timber. This is called deforestation and can lead to serious flooding.

Flooding and landslides

Without trees, land is at greater risk from flooding. This is because trees shield the land from sudden downpours and their roots take up water and help it soak into the ground. Without trees, water **erodes** the soil, increasing the risk of flooding.

Deforestation also increases the risk of landslides. After heavy rain, the soil becomes **saturated** with water and begins to slide downhill. Trees no longer provide a natural barrier to the moving soil.

Deforestation is a serious problem in many countries. Aid agencies encourage local people to plant new trees to replace the ones that were cut down. In this way, people protect their land from erosion and protect themselves from the risk of flooding and landslides.

▲ *When this forest was destroyed, thousands of tonnes of soil was washed away by rain.*

Paying the price

Some governments and international banks have lent money to **developing countries** for projects that destroy forests. These include projects to build dams and large farms to grow cash crops (left). Often these projects do not benefit local people, but only benefit the large companies who own the farms or build the dams. These projects mean that people are more at risk from flooding because their forests have been cleared.

Haiti 1997

Planting trees for the future

Haiti is the poorest country in the Caribbean. It is dominated by two large mountain ranges, where farmers have cleared forests to grow food crops.

Haiti has heavy downpours of rain between May and November, and towards the end of the rainy season it is often hit by **hurricanes**. The cutting down of trees on mountain slopes has eroded the soil and increased the risk of flooding in the valleys below.

But now a project has started which encourages children to replant trees on bare hillsides and so prevent these problems. It is run by a Haitian **environmental agency**, and is supported by the aid agency Save the Children Fund.

▲ *A hillside in Haiti shows signs of erosion after the trees were cut down.*

Benita, one of the children involved with the tree-planting project:

'We were told about the importance of trees to our environment, shown how to water them and how to protect them from animals that want to eat them... Now if I see someone cutting down a tree, I tell them that their actions affect us all.'

Benita shows off her seedlings which will reforest the hillsides.

RETURNING HOME

When flood water has subsided, people can return
to their homes. But they may need help to start again.

Picking up the pieces

Flood victims face many difficulties when they return
home. Their houses may have been torn down by the
torrent, their wells spoiled by dirty water and their crops
and animals killed. Everything they owned and worked
for may be damaged or lost. But within days, people start
picking up the pieces of their lives and are busy repairing
their homes or helping their neighbours.

Many people are too poor to replace the things they
lost in the flood, so governments and aid agencies help
people until they are able to carry on without aid. They
give out seeds for planting the next crop, or farm tools,
such as hoes, to work the land. Food aid may continue
until the next harvest.

Loan schemes

Some flood victims need
loans to restart local
businesses, such as basket
weaving, pottery or cloth
making. They need money
to buy materials or, if they
are fishermen, they need
new boats and nets. A loan
of money from a bank must
be repaid with interest.
Interest is an extra amount
that the person pays on top
of the money they have
borrowed. Aid agencies can
often give loans without the
extra charge on top. These
free loans allow the people
to buy what they need and
then pay back the money
over a period of time in
amounts they can afford.

◄ Villagers in the Philippines
clear away the mess after a flash
flood caused by deforestation.

Somalia 1997–98

Makeshift camps

Flooding began in this African country in October 1997 and continued well into 1998. By February 1998, nearly 2500 people had been killed and about one million people desperately needed help. Crops lay underwater, and as food supplies were used up, there was the risk of famine. So aid agencies made plans to give food aid to flood victims who had gathered together in makeshift camps on tiny patches of dry land.

The mother of a group of children made homeless by the flood told how they gathered materials for their makeshift hut:

'We gathered everything we could – pieces of metal sheeting, boards, uprooted bushes, and cardboard floating in the water.'

▲ *A view from the air showing a Somali village and surrounding fields swamped by the rising water.*

They had no clean drinking water and were surviving on fish and mangoes. Mosquitoes were spreading malaria. The Somali Red Crescent sprayed the village with **insecticides** to kill the mosquitoes, and set up a system to provide clean water.

▶ *A worker sprays insecticide over mosquito breeding areas.*

FLOOD DEFENCES

Countries at risk from flooding build flood defences
to hold back the water. But this can be expensive
and some countries cannot afford these costs.

Flood defences

River banks can be strengthened or raised
in parts. For example, high banks or levees
have been built along the Mississippi River
in the United States to protect people from
floods. Flood barriers are built across rivers
to protect cities from flooding. But these
defences are expensive. Aid agencies help
poorer countries to protect themselves.
River banks are raised and **spillways** are
dug to divert high water from where it will
cause most damage.

Many countries have storm shelters
where people can go if waters start rising. They are built of
brick and plaster and are raised on columns to withstand
wind, rain and flood water.

▲ *Bangladeshi women work
to build an embankment.*

Repairing the damage

Floods damage roads and bridges, weaken buildings, wash away fences and trees
and leave debris everywhere. Repairing large structures takes time and effort, and
not all building materials are available locally. Aid agencies can help by sending
materials, such as concrete and bricks, to the affected area. But it is usually local
people who clean up the mess after the flood and
organize the repairs to be carried out (left). If necessary,
aid agencies support them with cash-for-work schemes
which pay people for the repair work they do.

Bangladesh 1997

Cyclone shelters

Bangladesh is a low-lying country in Asia which is often hit by tropical storms called cyclones. Cyclones whip up huge waves at sea which cause much damage and may kill many people when they come ashore. A cyclone in 1991, for example, killed 13 000 people. In May 1997, another cyclone struck Bangladesh. It was as powerful as the 1991 storm, and destroyed or damaged 400 000 homes, but it killed less people. Around 200 people died. This is because people took refuge in cyclone shelters while the storm raged. Many of the shelters were built with help from aid agencies, such as ACTIONAID.

▲ *Flooding caused by a cyclone. Every year these powerful storms threaten Bangladesh.*

Nur Begum and her family run a small roadside restaurant serving customers rotis (a round, flat bread) and tea. They took refuge in a shelter when the cyclone hit:

'We had to stay there for two days because the area became flooded with sea water. The storm damaged the roof of our roadside restaurant and the oven we used to cook the rotis.'

Children stand outside a cyclone shelter. It was built with the help of the aid agencies.

MANAGING FLOODS

A plan of action helps countries at risk from flooding to react swiftly when disaster strikes.

Action plans

Countries all over the world are affected by natural disasters, such as floods, earthquakes, droughts and volcanic eruptions.

For people who live in these countries, the threat of natural disasters is a part of everyday life, so it is better if they know what to do if disaster strikes. Aid agencies and governments work together to draw up disaster rescue plans.

These plans start by looking at the hazards a country faces and producing a map of the areas most at risk. A system for warning about the arrival of a disaster is put into place. Emergency services are taught what to do if disaster strikes, such as how to reach flood victims and how to treat them for **hypothermia**. Measures are taken, such as building storm shelters, to prevent the worst effects of a flood.

The plan also includes telling people about the work that is being done to protect them, and giving them advice about what they should do if a flood strikes.

Getting ready

Here are some of the things people are advised to do if their area is hit by a flood: to listen to the radio for news about the flood and advice about what to do; to disconnect televisions and other electrical devices; to move valuable belongings and clothes out of reach of the water; to help move vehicles and farm animals to high ground; to prevent pollution by moving dangerous chemicals, such as insecticides, to a safe place; to turn off electricity and gas supplies and to lock windows and doors when leaving home; to return home only when the level of the water has subsided; not to wander around flooded areas alone.

◄ *A Chinese woman is helped to safety by soldiers.*

Pacific Islands 1998
Reducing the damage

The islands of the South Pacific, such as the Solomon Islands, Cook Islands, Fiji and Papua New Guinea, are beautiful islands with palm-fringed beaches. But they are regularly threatened by disasters that can kill people and destroy homes.

Cyclones are the most common disasters and have the most damaging effect. They whip up the sea to create huge waves that crash ashore, damaging or destroying everything in their path. The wind also causes damage, and dangerous mudslides may follow the heavy rains.

► *The human-made reef around Kurumba Island in the Maldives is designed to protect it against rising sea levels.*

▼ *Upolu Island in Western Samoa is lashed by high winds and crashing waves during a powerful tropical storm.*

In 1994, the island countries and the United Nations worked together to reduce the effects of natural disasters in the area. They set up a scheme for disaster management, called the South Pacific Disaster Reduction Programme (SDRP), which includes flood warning and forecasting, training of officials, providing the public with information on what to do if disaster strikes, and closer contact between the islands of the South Pacific.

HOW YOU CAN HELP

Floods are a danger in many countries, large and small, rich and poor. Sometimes, people lose everything they own in a flood.

● Collect newspaper cuttings about floods and mark on a map where they happened. Did aid agencies send relief supplies to the country affected?

● Find out about an aid agency you would like to help. With your friends, collect unwanted books, clothes and blankets and donate them to your chosen charity.

● You might like to raise money for your charity by organizing a fundraising activity. A sponsored swim or run is fun for everyone. Perhaps your whole school could be involved. You could design your own sponsorship forms and give information about how the money will be spent.

Finding out more

Write to aid agencies or visit their web sites to find out about their work and how you can help.

British Red Cross
9 Grosvenor Crescent
London SW1X 7EJ
Telephone: 0171 235 5454
http://www.redcross.org.uk

OXFAM
274 Banbury Road
Oxford OX2 7DZ
Telephone: 01865 313600
http://www.oxfam.org.uk

Save the Children Fund (SCF)
17 Grove Lane
London SE5 8RD
Telephone: 0171 703 5400
http://www.oneworld.org/scf/

ACTIONAID
Hamlyn House
Macdonald Road
Archway
London N19 5PG
Telephone: 0171 281 4101
http://www.oneworld.org/actionaid

Médecins Sans Frontières (MSF)
124–132 Clerkenwell Road
London EC1R 5DL
Telephone: 0171 713 5600
http://www.msf.orge

The Office for the Coordination of Humanitarian Affairs (OCHA)
http://www.reliefweb.int

The International Federation of Red Cross and Red Crescent Societies
17 chemin des Crêts
Petit-Saconnex
PO Box 372
CH-1211
Geneva 19
Switzerland
Telephone: 00 41 22 730 4222
http://www.ifrc.org

GLOSSARY

aid agency An organization that helps people when there is a disaster and runs long-term projects to help people in poorer countries.

amphibious Vehicle designed for both land and water.

debris Remains of something that has been broken or destroyed.

developing countries The poorer countries of the world that are using their resources to increase the standard of living of their people.

drought A long period of time without rainfall.

dykes Embankments or walls built to prevent flooding or to keep out the sea.

environmental agency An organization that helps people to live in harmony with the land and to protect it.

erosion The wearing away of the soil by sea water or rain.

European Union A group of European countries who work together.

evacuated Moved from a place of danger to a place of safety.

Hercules A type of large plane designed for transporting heavy loads.

hurricanes Severe storms with high winds and heavy rain.

hypothermia Very low body temperature due to the cold which can be fatal.

insecticides Chemicals used to kill insects that spread disease or destroy crops.

landslides Large amounts of soil and rock which slide down a hill, usually after a heavy rainfall.

malnutrition Weakness of the body through lack of food or not eating the right kinds of food.

Médecins Sans Frontières (MSF) An aid agency which offers medical help in a crisis. The name is French for 'doctors without borders'.

mosquito A small flying insect that feeds on the blood of humans and animals.

orbit The path of a satellite as it travels around the earth.

Red Cross An international aid agency which was set up in 1863.

saturated Soil that has become completely soaked with water.

sewers Drains or pipes that carry away waste material from homes.

Soviet Union A large country in Eastern Europe and Asia, formed of many different states. The Soviet Union split apart in 1991.

spillways Channels that carry away water when a river floods.

state of emergency When a government announces that it will use the emergency services and army to rescue disaster victims.

torrents Fast-flowing water.

typhoons Violent storms.

United Nations (UN) An organization of countries around the world which encourages world peace and offers help to people in a crisis.

volunteers People who are willing to come forward and help when a disaster strikes.

INDEX

First published in Great Britain in 1999 by

Chrysalis Children's Books
An imprint of Chrysalis Books Group plc
The Chrysalis Building, Bramley Road,
London W10 6SP

Copyright in this format © Chrysalis Books Group plc 1999
Text copyright © Paul Bennet 1999

Paperback edition published in 2003

Series editor Julie Hill
Series designer Simeen Karim
Consultants Dr Peter Walker and Elizabeth Bassant
Picture researcher Diana Morris

ISBN 1 85561 811 7 (hb)
ISBN 1 84138 952 8 (pb)

British Library Cataloguing in Publication Data
for this book is available from the British Library.

Printed in Hong Kong

Photographic credits

Saeed Ahmed/Associated Press: 16t. Tantyo Bangun/Still Pictures: 10b. Michel Bonnaventure/Sipa Press/Rex Features: 6t. British Red Cross: 7t, 7b, 19b Paul Stewart. Chine Nouvelle-Sipa Press/Rex Features: 4, 28. Nigel Dickinson/Still Pictures: 24t. Jean-Léo Dugast/Panos: 23t. Mark Edwards/Still Pictures: 22t. Grabka/Action Press/Rex Features:15b. G. Griffiths-Christian Aid/Still Pictures: title page, 17t. Paul Harrison/Still Pictures: 12b. Jeremy Hartley/Panos: 16b. Jim Holmes/Environmental Images: 18b, 20t. Jim Holmes/Panos: 9b, 27b. Fred Hoogervorst/Panos: 22b. ICRC: 25b Clive Shirley. L.A DailyNews/Liaison/Gamma/Frank Spooner Pictures: front cover. Topi Lyambila/Associated Press: 17b. Y. Maecke/Gaff/Sipa Press/Rex Features: 15t. Maitland-Titterton/Rex Features: back cover. Martin Mejia/Associated Press: 11b. Miladinovic/Sipa Press/Rex Features: contents page & 6b. Gemma Miralda/Associated Press: 11t. Steve Morgan/Environmental Images: 10t. Gerard & Margi Moss/Still Pictures: 29b. Gil Moti/Still Pictures: 13t, 13b. NASA/Still Pictures: 8t. Anne Nosten/Gamma/Frank Spooner Pictures: 25t. Trevor Page/Panos: 19t, 26b. Noel Quidu/Gamma/Frank Spooner Pictures:21b. Laurent Rebours/Associated Press: 21t. R. Roberts/Sipa Press/Rex Features:14t.Cyril Ruoso/Still Pictures: 8b. David J. Sams/Sipa Press/Rex Features: 12t.Dominic Sansoni/Environmental Images: 29t. Save the Children Fund: 23b Julio Etchart. Jorgen Schytte/Still Pictures:26t. Sipa Press/Rex Features: 27t. Liba Taylor/Panos: 18t. Richard Vogel/ Associated Press: 9t.